Turning PLR into Gold

Turning PLR into Gold

Strategies for Maximum Profitability

Jennifer Jackman

Bald and Bonkers Network Academy

CONTENTS

First Printing, 2024

ISBN: 979-8-8692-5936-3
EISBN: 979-8-8692-5937-0

Editing assistance for this book was provided by artificial intelligence technology.

1

An Introduction To Private Label Rights Content

Private label rights content has revolutionized the process of selling products online by offering a streamlined approach that eliminates the need for extensive content creation. This method significantly reduces the time and effort required to develop original material, making it particularly advantageous for individuals who are not inclined towards structured writing.

It is crucial, however, to customize the acquired

content before finalizing it for distribution. Merely purchasing private label rights content is not sufficient; the key lies in enhancing its quality and structure during the modification process. The profitability of your endeavors will depend on how effectively you refine and present the content to your audience.

Quantity alone does not guarantee success when utilizing private label content. Selling a large volume of copies does not ensure profitability if the content lacks substance and relevance. Ensuring that your content is well-structured, informative, and tailored to meet the needs of your target audience significantly increases your chances of maximizing profits and minimizing potential refund requests.

In today's digital age, while vast amounts of information are freely available online, consumers value convenience and instant access. Many prefer to pay for readily available information rather than spending hours searching for it themselves. As a content provider, you can capitalize on this demand by offering instant access to valuable information that addresses your audience's needs effectively.

Quality content remains paramount in driving lucrative profits in the information era. Consumers seek valuable and timely information, and by delivering it in a compelling and informative manner, you can establish yourself as a trusted source and attract paying customers.

Utilizing private label content streamlines the process of acquiring information and allows for customization to suit your specific requirements. While selling private label rights content can be profitable, offering unique and original content commands higher value and enhances your revenue potential. Customers value exclusivity and are willing to pay more for content that is not widely available or recycled. By focusing on creating and selling unique content, you can establish a sustainable and profitable business model in the digital marketplace.

Furthermore, selling unique content provides

additional opportunities for revenue generation. Unlike selling private label rights content multiple times, unique content ownership transfers to the buyer, allowing you to charge premium prices. This exclusivity adds value and appeal to your offerings, attracting customers who seek original and distinctive content.

The appeal of unique content extends beyond monetary gains. It also establishes your brand as a trusted authority in your niche, fostering customer loyalty and repeat business. Customers value authenticity and originality, and by consistently delivering unique content that meets their needs, you can build a loyal customer base and increase your profitability over time.

In conclusion, the strategic use of private label rights content, coupled with the creation and sale of unique content, offers a potent combination for maximizing profits in the digital landscape. By focusing on quality, customization, and exclusivity, you can differentiate yourself in the market, attract a loyal customer following, and achieve sustainable long-term success.

2

The Explanation Of Private Label Rights

Private Label Rights (PLR) has emerged as a significant asset in the realm of internet marketing, offering a wealth of opportunities for individuals seeking to develop new products and content. This versatile content can be sold to others and customized according to the buyer's preferences, allowing for flexibility in editing sentences, paragraphs, and other elements as desired.

However, it's essential to note that some creators may impose limitations on the use of PLR content, affecting the extent to which it can be edited. Prior to purchasing PLR content, it's advisable to clarify the terms with the seller to avoid any constraints that may hinder your editing capabilities.

Typically, PLR content is delivered in formats such as .doc (document), .rtf (rich text file), or .txt (text file), making it accessible for editing in programs like Microsoft Word or Notepad. While you can attribute authorship to yourself, it's recommended to make substantial changes to differentiate the content from its original form.

Customizing PLR content goes beyond changing the authorship; it involves reviewing and enhancing the content to align with your objectives and target audience. This may include rephrasing paragraphs, substituting words, and ensuring clarity without resorting to overly complex language.

The purpose of modifying PLR content is to create unique and valuable material that stands out in a competitive market. By avoiding duplication and offering fresh perspectives, you enhance the value and appeal of your products. This extends to crafting compelling titles and headlines that captivate readers' attention and convey the essence of your content effectively.

Ultimately, the goal is to elevate the quality and relevance of your offerings, ensuring they resonate with your audience and differentiate your brand in a crowded marketplace. Thought-provoking titles and well-crafted content not only attract attention but also establish credibility and drive engagement, leading to enhanced success and profitability.

Additionally, standing out from competitors requires more than just superficial modifications to PLR content. It's crucial to infuse substance into the body of your content, making it both informative and engaging for your audience. This involves identifying areas where the content can be expanded upon or enriched to provide a more comprehensive and valuable experience for readers.

Furthermore, don't overlook the importance of titles and headlines. These elements serve as the first point of contact with potential customers, influencing their decision to engage with your content. A well-crafted title or headline that sparks curiosity and conveys the benefits of your content can significantly impact its success.

Consider the difference between a generic title like "Tips to Revive Your Marriage" and a compelling one such as "10 Tips To Revive Your Marriage Before You End Up In Divorce Court." The latter not only grabs attention but also communicates urgency and a solution to a pressing problem, enticing readers to delve deeper into the content.

Ultimately, the key to maximizing the value of PLR content lies in your ability to transform it into something unique, valuable, and appealing to your target audience. By investing time and effort into thoughtful editing, content enrichment, and impactful titles, you can differentiate your offerings, attract more customers, and achieve greater success in the competitive digital landscape.

3

Terms For Private Label Rights Content

It is prudent to seek profitability through private label rights (PLR) content, as it can yield lucrative returns. However, it's imperative to operate within the parameters set forth by the content seller. Copyright laws are applicable from the moment content is created, necessitating a thorough understanding and adherence to the seller's terms.

When engaging in transactions involving PLR content, carefully review and comprehend the seller's terms to avoid potential legal issues. Failure to comply with these terms can lead to significant repercussions.

Here are some common considerations that sellers may establish when outlining terms for PLR content:

1. ***Selling Rights:*** Sellers typically permit the resale of PLR packages to others. However, this can lead to devaluation if buyers simply resell the content without making substantial modifications to differentiate it.
2. ***Packaging Options:*** Some sellers allow PLR content to be bundled with related materials for resale, while others may restrict such packaging to maintain content value.
3. ***Content Modification:*** Modifying PLR content is essential to creating uniqueness and maximizing profitability. This differentiation is crucial to stand out from competitors who opt for unaltered content.
4. ***Giveaway Permissions:*** Offering PLR content as a giveaway can contribute to

devaluation, leading some sellers to opt out of this option.

5. ***Bonus Offerings:*** Sellers may permit PLR content to be offered as a bonus with other products, though this can be contentious due to potential devaluation concerns.
6. ***Paid Membership Sites:*** Some sellers avoid offering PLR content to paid membership sites to control distribution and maintain content value.
7. ***Resale and Master Resale Rights:*** Certain sellers allow resale and master resale rights, expanding the potential for revenue generation.
8. ***Selling of PLR Rights:*** Selling PLR rights directly is often prohibited by sellers to protect content value and avoid price devaluation.
9. ***Auction Sites:*** Selling PLR content on auction sites can rapidly devalue the content, leading sellers to restrict such sales to maintain content integrity and value.

Occasionally, sellers may offer unrestricted PLR

rights, providing unparalleled freedom to distribute or modify the content as desired. Understanding these terms enables you to make informed decisions that align with your profitability goals.

By selecting terms that optimize profitability and preserve content value, you can enhance your bottom line and capitalize on the potential of PLR content effectively.

Furthermore, navigating these terms allows you to strategize and implement approaches that maximize your profits effectively. Consider the following factors to determine which terms align best with your business objectives and financial goals:

1. ***Value Preservation:*** Choose terms that prioritize the preservation of content value and integrity. Avoid options that may lead to rapid devaluation, such as unrestricted resale rights or selling PLR rights at low prices.
2. ***Differentiation:*** Emphasize the importance of modifying PLR content to create unique offerings that stand out in the

market. Opt for terms that encourage customization and discourage "cookie-cutter" approaches.

3. ***Targeted Distribution:*** Evaluate options for distributing PLR content strategically. Determine whether offering it as a bonus, through membership sites, or in bundled packages complements your overall marketing strategy and audience targeting.
4. ***Legal Compliance:*** Ensure strict adherence to copyright laws and seller terms to mitigate legal risks. Clarify any uncertainties with sellers before proceeding with distribution or resale.
5. ***Marketplace Dynamics:*** Consider the impact of marketplace dynamics, such as competition on auction sites or saturation of certain niches with PLR content. Make informed decisions based on market trends and demand.
6. ***Long-Term Sustainability:*** Focus on building a sustainable business model by selecting terms that support long-term profitability and customer satisfaction. Prioritize

value creation and customer engagement over short-term gains that may compromise content quality.

Ultimately, leveraging PLR content for profitability requires a strategic approach that balances commercial objectives with ethical and legal considerations. By understanding and leveraging seller terms effectively, you can harness the full potential of PLR content to drive revenue growth and establish a competitive advantage in your industry.

4

Why Private Label Rights Are A Lucrative Business

Private label rights (PLR) present an invaluable opportunity for individuals who may not possess strong authorship or writing skills. This option allows them to acquire pre-written content without the need for extensive creative effort, making it particularly appealing for those looking to streamline their content creation process. However, as previously mentioned, it's crucial to customize the PLR content to ensure uniqueness and relevance to your target audience. This customization extends beyond mere editing; it involves adding your own insights, perspectives, and value propositions to make the content truly stand out.

Furthermore, changing the title of the PLR content can significantly enhance its appeal and marketability. A captivating and relevant title not only attracts attention but also communicates the essence of your product effectively. It serves as a powerful tool for branding and differentiation in a crowded marketplace, helping you establish a distinct identity and attract potential customers.

One of the primary advantages of utilizing PLR content is its cost-effectiveness. Unlike hiring expensive ghostwriters or outsourcing writing tasks, PLR content can be obtained at a fraction of the cost, making it a budget-friendly option for content creation. However, it's essential to note that for more complex projects such as software development or scripting, specialized expertise may be required. In such cases, hiring a professional at a reasonable price can streamline the process and ensure quality outcomes.

To find suitable professionals for specialized tasks, reputable internet marketing forums and platforms can be a valuable resource. These platforms often feature experienced professionals offering their services at competitive rates. By leveraging these resources, you can access the expertise needed to enhance your PLR content and create compelling products that resonate with your audience.

Emphasizing originality and uniqueness in your product offerings is key to success in today's competitive market. Modern consumers seek personalized and innovative solutions, avoiding generic "cookie-cutter" products. By differentiating your products through customization, you demonstrate a commitment to quality and customer satisfaction, ultimately earning trust and loyalty from your audience.

Leveraging PLR content effectively involves not only customizing and enhancing the content but also strategically positioning it with compelling titles and branding. By taking these steps, you can maximize the potential of PLR content to drive profitability and success in your business endeavors.

Additionally, the versatility of PLR content extends beyond traditional written material. Many PLR providers offer multimedia content such as videos, audio files, graphics, and templates, providing a wide range of options to create diverse and engaging products. Incorporating multimedia elements into your offerings can enhance the overall user experience and appeal to different learning preferences, further boosting the marketability of your products.

Moreover, the scalability of PLR content allows you to expand your product line quickly and efficiently. By leveraging existing PLR materials and customizing them to suit various niches or audience segments, you can create a portfolio of products that cater to different needs and preferences. This diversity not only increases your revenue potential but also strengthens your brand's presence in the market.

Furthermore, PLR content offers a time-saving solution for entrepreneurs and businesses. Instead of spending hours or days creating content from scratch, you can leverage PLR materials as a foundation and focus your time and energy on strategic tasks such as marketing, customer engagement, and product development. This efficient use of resources enables you to scale your business effectively and stay ahead of the competition.

In today's digital landscape, where content consumption is rapidly evolving, PLR content provides a flexible and adaptable solution to meet changing market demands. By staying updated with the latest trends and insights in your industry, you can leverage PLR content to create timely and relevant products that resonate with your audience.

Ultimately, the key to success with PLR content lies in strategic planning, customization, and innovative marketing strategies. By harnessing the full potential of PLR materials and aligning them with your business goals, you can unlock new opportunities for growth, profitability, and long-term success in your ventures.

5

Types Of Private Label Rights Content

Various types of private label rights (PLR) content offer profitable opportunities for entrepreneurs. PLR content goes beyond traditional articles and reports in document or rich text formats; it encompasses software and scripts that can generate substantial income.

Articles are widely available in the PLR market, accessible through forums, dedicated websites, and membership sites. While membership sites may offer a variety of products, including articles, some entrepreneurs prefer specialized platforms solely focused on articles for ease of selection.

Membership sites have gained popularity, offering monthly subscriptions ranging from $10 to $97, with higher prices often indicating better quality content and additional benefits. However, entrepreneurs with budget constraints can explore free PLR article sites, although these may require more editing.

E-books and reports are another lucrative format for PLR content. They offer versatility, allowing entrepreneurs to create standalone products or repurpose content into smaller reports. Dividing longer e-books into smaller reports can appeal to audiences with limited time or interest in comprehensive reads.

Membership sites also provide access to e-books with PLR rights, offering reasonably priced monthly subscriptions. However, the uncertainty of future content releases can be a consideration for subscribers.

Software with PLR rights presents a significant revenue opportunity, often surpassing earnings from e-book sales. Entrepreneurs can develop or commission various software programs for resale, tapping into a high-demand market.

Scripts, a form of web-based software, are easily editable and deployable on websites, making them a convenient choice for customization and utilization.

Another aspect of PLR is public domain content, comprising material published before 1923 without copyright claims. Entrepreneurs should verify public domain status through reputable sources, ensuring legality and avoiding potential copyright issues.

Membership sites specializing in public domain content can provide licensed material for modification and resale. Platforms like Gutenberg offer a wealth of public domain material, although caution is advised to ensure compliance with usage regulations.

Utilizing PLR and public domain content strategically can lead to significant profitability, offering a range of products to meet diverse market demands and preferences. However, thorough research and adherence to legal guidelines are essential to maximize the benefits of these content types.

Entrepreneurs looking to capitalize on PLR and public domain content must navigate the nuances of each type to harness their full potential for profit generation.

Public domain content, particularly from reputable sources like Gutenberg, offers a treasure trove of material that can be freely used and modified to create unique products. However, it's crucial to conduct thorough checks to ensure that the material falls within the public domain guidelines. Some content may have specific usage restrictions based on publication dates or other factors, requiring careful assessment before utilization.

Membership sites specializing in public domain content can be a valuable resource, provided they are properly licensed and transparent about their offerings. Look for indications of legal involvement, such as attorney oversight, to ensure the legitimacy of the content and your rights to modify and distribute it.

In addition to public domain content, PLR materials in the form of articles, e-books, software, and scripts offer diverse opportunities for revenue generation. Entrepreneurs can leverage PLR content to create a range of products tailored to different audience preferences and market segments.

When using PLR content, it's essential to focus on customization and value addition. Simply repackaging PLR content without significant modifications may lead to a lack of differentiation and reduced appeal to customers. By adding unique insights, updates, or enhancements, entrepreneurs can transform PLR content into high-quality offerings that command premium prices and attract loyal customers.

Moreover, entrepreneurs should explore creative ways to monetize PLR and public domain content beyond direct sales. This could include offering resell or master resell rights, bundling products into comprehensive packages, creating membership sites or courses, or leveraging content for lead generation and marketing purposes.

Ultimately, success with PLR and public domain content hinges on a strategic approach that balances legality, customization, and market demand. By staying informed, ethically using the content, and delivering value to customers, entrepreneurs can unlock the full potential of these resources and drive sustainable profits in their businesses.

6

Other Enhancements To Make Your Private Label Content Unique

When purchasing a private label rights (PLR) package that includes headers, graphics, and a sales page, it's essential to consider customizing the images to create a unique and professional appearance. Customers are increasingly seeking originality and high-quality design elements that set products apart from standard "cookie-cutter" offerings.

Often, the graphics included in PLR packages

may not meet the desired standards in terms of appeal or visual clarity. Subpar graphics can detract from the professionalism of a website and may deter potential buyers. To address this, entrepreneurs can opt to have custom graphics professionally created by experienced graphic artists.

Internet marketing forums often feature skilled graphic designers offering competitive rates, ranging from $37 upwards depending on the scope of work. Negotiating a fair price for customized graphics can enhance the overall visual appeal of your products and significantly impact customer perception.

For entrepreneurs with budget constraints, Adobe Photoshop offers a 30-day trial period, providing access to top-tier graphics software for creating high-quality visuals. This option allows for the creation of captivating graphics that align with your brand identity and elevate your online presence.

In addition to graphics, revising the copy on

sales pages is crucial for differentiation and attracting buyers. Tailoring the sales page content to reflect your unique value proposition and brand voice can distinguish your offerings from competitors and increase customer engagement.

While hiring an experienced copywriter is beneficial, entrepreneurs can still improve their copywriting skills through self-study using reputable copywriting manuals or by analyzing and learning from successful sales pages in their niche. However, it's crucial to avoid directly copying content from other sales pages to avoid potential copyright infringement issues.

By investing time and effort in customizing graphics and refining sales page copy, entrepreneurs can create a compelling and distinctive online presence that resonates with their target audience and drives sales effectively.

Furthermore, making strategic changes to the wording and layout of the sales pages is paramount in establishing a unique and compelling online presence. This customization not only differentiates your offerings from competitors but also enhances the overall user experience, leading to increased sales conversions.

While hiring an experienced copywriter is advantageous, entrepreneurs with budget constraints can still improve their copywriting skills through self-study. Utilizing reputable copywriting manuals or studying successful sales pages in similar niches can provide valuable insights into effective copywriting techniques and persuasive messaging.

It's important to note that directly copying content from other sales pages is not only unethical but also poses legal risks, including potential copyright infringement issues. Instead, focus on understanding the key elements of persuasive copywriting, such as addressing customer pain points, highlighting benefits, and creating a sense of urgency or exclusivity.

Additionally, conducting thorough research on customer preferences, market trends, and competitor strategies can inform your copywriting approach and help you craft compelling sales messages that resonate with your target audience.

In conclusion, customizing graphics and refining sales page copy are essential steps in optimizing the effectiveness of PLR packages and creating a distinctive brand identity. By investing time and effort in these areas, entrepreneurs can elevate their online presence, attract more customers, and achieve greater success in their business endeavors.

7

Different Ways To Brand Your Private Label Rights Content

Branding your private label rights (PLR) product can significantly enhance its appeal and marketability, allowing you to establish a unique identity and increase recognition among your target audience. There are several strategic approaches you can adopt to effectively brand your PLR product and set it apart from generic offerings:

1. ***Personalized Title:*** One of the simplest yet impactful ways to brand your PLR

product is by adding your name to the title. For instance, instead of a generic title like "Strategies For Online Profits," you could personalize it as "Jane Smith's Strategies For Online Profits." This not only adds a personal touch but also establishes you as the authoritative figure behind the content, instilling trust and credibility among potential buyers.

2. ***Incorporating a Logo:*** Another effective branding strategy is to include a logo that represents you or your company. A well-designed logo can convey professionalism, reliability, and a sense of identity. You can create a logo using graphic design software that offers logo templates or enlist the services of a skilled graphic designer to craft a custom logo that aligns with your brand image and values.
3. ***Creating a Series:*** Consider creating a series of PLR products under a specific name or theme, such as the "Wealthy Business" series. This approach not only adds coherence and continuity to your product

line but also helps you build a recognizable brand identity in your niche. Customers are more likely to recognize and trust a series of products that consistently deliver value and expertise in a particular area.

In addition to these branding strategies, it's essential to maintain consistency across your PLR products in terms of design elements, tone of voice, and messaging. Consistency reinforces your brand identity and fosters a sense of familiarity and trust among your audience.

Moreover, leverage your branding efforts across various marketing channels, including your website, social media profiles, email campaigns, and promotional materials. Consistent branding across these platforms reinforces your brand image and strengthens brand recall among potential customers.

By implementing these branding strategies and maintaining consistency in your marketing efforts, you can effectively differentiate your PLR products, establish a strong brand presence, and attract loyal customers who resonate with your brand values and offerings.

8

Ideas And Strategies For Maximum PLR Profits Revealed

Viral Marketing Strategy:

Viral marketing operates akin to a contagion, spreading rapidly among audiences, but in a positive light. Leveraging your private label rights (PLR) materials for viral marketing can yield substantial benefits. One effective approach is offering freebies to your subscriber list, such as a report crafted from your PLR content or complimentary software tools. The allure of "free" is potent in marketing, drawing people like magnets to such offerings.

Encouraging your subscribers to share these freebies with others can exponentially expand your reach. As more people join your list and discover the quality of your offerings, they are more inclined to become paying customers, leading to increased revenue. This strategy underscores the principle of reciprocity—by providing value upfront, you cultivate a loyal customer base willing to invest in your products or services.

Affiliate Links Integration:

Integrating affiliate links strategically into your free reports can also be a lucrative tactic. However, it's crucial to strike a balance and avoid overwhelming the report with excessive affiliate promotions. Overloading the report with too many affiliate links can dilute its value and come across as overly sales-oriented, potentially deterring potential subscribers.

To maintain professionalism and reader engagement, consider cloaking affiliate links discreetly. This ensures that the focus remains on delivering valuable content to readers, with affiliate promotions seamlessly integrated for interested parties. Crafting compelling copy that emphasizes the benefits of the products or services linked can also enhance conversion rates, maximizing your affiliate earnings.

Expert Interviews for Value Addition:

Enhancing the value of your PLR product can be achieved through expert interviews. Collaborating with industry experts to provide insights related to your niche adds credibility and depth to your product. By incorporating expert opinions and advice, you enrich the content, making it more informative and appealing to your target audience.

Highlighting these interviews in your product enhances its perceived value, positioning you as a trusted authority in your field. This, coupled with your modifications to the PLR content, creates a unique and valuable resource that resonates with customers, driving sales and profitability.

Utilizing Free Audio Content:

Instead of traditional e-books, consider leveraging your PLR content to create free audio content. By transforming your content into engaging audio formats, you cater to different audience preferences and enhance accessibility. Additionally, customizing the content to reflect your unique perspective and insights adds value and distinguishes your offerings from generic alternatives.

Offering free audio content as a lead magnet for newsletter opt-ins can significantly expand your subscriber base. The perceived value of original audio content entices prospects to join your list, opening avenues for future sales and business growth. This strategy capitalizes on the allure of "free" while showcasing your expertise and establishing rapport with potential customers.

Utilizing E-Bay Strategically:

While direct sales of original PLR products on platforms like E-Bay may not be feasible due to potential devaluation, strategic modifications can overcome these challenges. Modifying the products extensively, including title enhancements and value additions, makes them more appealing and distinct in a competitive market.

Utilize your E-Bay profile's "About Me" section effectively by linking to your opt-in page or related products. This indirect approach encourages engagement and list building while adhering to platform regulations. By showcasing your modified PLR products creatively, you can attract interested buyers and channel them towards your sales funnel, maximizing profitability.

Leveraging Content for Newsletters and E-Courses:

Private label rights articles serve as valuable content sources for newsletters and e-courses. However, mere replication without modification can lead to generic content and diminished engagement.

Customizing the PLR content to align with your brand voice and audience preferences enhances its relevance and impact.

Incorporate fresh insights, examples, and analyses to elevate the content's quality and distinctiveness. By offering unique and valuable content in your newsletters and e-courses, you position yourself as an authority, fostering trust and loyalty among subscribers. This trust translates into increased sales opportunities and sustained profitability.

Exploring Article Pack Websites and Small Reports Creation:

Article pack websites and small reports creation offer lucrative avenues for monetizing your PLR content. Conduct thorough market research to identify trending topics and audience preferences. Tailor your content offerings to address these interests, ensuring relevance and appeal.

Crafting small reports from modified PLR

articles allows you to showcase your expertise and provide targeted solutions to audience needs. Focus on creating engaging titles and informative content that sets your reports apart from competitors. By addressing specific pain points and delivering actionable insights, you enhance the reports' value and sales potential.

Harnessing the full potential of your PLR content requires strategic planning, creative modifications, and targeted marketing efforts. By leveraging various platforms and formats, such as viral marketing, affiliate links integration, expert interviews, free audio content, E-Bay optimization, newsletter content, e-courses, article pack websites, and small reports creation, you can maximize profitability and establish a strong brand presence in your niche.

Creating compelling and engaging small reports can significantly boost your sales and profits. Here are some effective titles to consider:

1. 7 Ways To Slim Down In A Matter Of Months
2. 5 Ways To Boost Your Self-Esteem And Eliminate Negativity
3. 10 Tips to Save On Your Wedding And Avoid Financial Stress
4. How To De-Stress And Achieve a Balanced Life
5. Strategies for Building an Engaged Mailing List
6. Effective Solutions for Clearing Acne from Your Skin

Small reports have a distinct advantage in the market as they are easier to sell due to their concise nature. Unlike lengthy e-books that require time to read, small reports can be consumed in one sitting, making them more appealing to buyers. Even if a customer's expectations are not fully met, they are likely to keep the report rather than seeking a refund for a nominal price.

Moreover, bundling small reports can create

additional value for customers and drive more sales. Offering a bundle of related reports at a special price, such as five reports for $37, can entice customers to opt for the bundled offer, leading to increased profits for you.

Physical products derived from private label rights content also present lucrative opportunities. By modifying and repurposing the content, you can create CDs, DVDs, and printed books. These physical products hold a higher perceived value among consumers, especially those who prefer audio and video formats over e-books.

Creating audio content is relatively simple, requiring just a microphone and free software like Audacity. Video content, on the other hand, can be produced using tools like Camtasia, offering a dynamic and engaging way to deliver information. These formats are preferred by many as they allow for a more immersive learning experience compared to traditional e-books.

Selling physical products on platforms like E-

Bay and Cafepress can further expand your reach and profitability. Home study courses packaged with modified private label content can also command higher prices and attract discerning customers looking for comprehensive learning materials.

Additionally, implementing master resell rights strategies can generate upfront profits by offering bundled products with resale rights to your subscribers. This not only boosts sales but also expands your mailing list and establishes you as an authority in your niche.

Incorporating bum marketing techniques, which involve article marketing and promoting products through articles, can also yield long-term profits. By leveraging private label rights articles and modifying them for uniqueness, you can create a steady stream of traffic and sales over time.

Overall, modifying private label rights content to create diverse products and implementing effective marketing strategies can lead to substantial profits and establish your brand as a trusted authority in your industry.

Furthermore, exploring various avenues for distributing and promoting your modified private label rights products can significantly enhance your profits and market reach.

Utilizing online marketplaces such as ClickBank can be a strategic move to promote and sell your products. Conduct thorough research to identify high-converting products in your niche with attractive commission rates. Aligning your private label rights articles with these products can create a cohesive marketing strategy that drives sales and commissions.

When submitting articles for bum marketing, it's crucial to focus on creating unique and valuable content. Search engines and article directories favor original content that provides valuable insights to readers. By leveraging modified private label rights articles and customizing them to meet the specific needs of your target audience, you can attract more traffic and potential customers.

Additionally, incorporating multimedia elements such as videos and podcasts can further enhance your marketing efforts. Video tutorials, product demonstrations, and expert interviews can add depth and credibility to your offerings, enticing customers to make purchases.

Social media platforms offer immense opportunities for promoting your modified private label rights products. Engage with your audience through compelling content, interactive posts, and targeted advertisements. Leveraging social proof, such as customer testimonials and success stories, can build trust and credibility, leading to increased sales and repeat business.

Email marketing remains a powerful tool for driving conversions and nurturing customer relationships. Create engaging email campaigns that highlight the value and benefits of your products. Offer exclusive discounts, bonuses, and valuable content to incentivize purchases and encourage customer loyalty.

Collaborating with influencers and industry experts can also amplify your marketing efforts. Partnering with influencers who align with your brand values and target audience can help you reach a wider audience and gain credibility within your niche.

Furthermore, continuous monitoring and optimization of your marketing strategies are essential for long-term success. Analyze metrics such as conversion rates, click-through rates, and customer feedback to identify areas for improvement and refine your approach.

By leveraging the power of modified private label rights content and implementing effective marketing strategies across various channels, you can maximize profits, expand your market presence, and build a strong and sustainable business in your chosen niche.

Expanding your revenue streams through strategic approaches like firesales can be a highly effective strategy when leveraging private label rights content. Firesales involve bundling multiple products created from private label rights content and offering them at varying prices over a set period.

The pricing structure typically starts at a lower rate, such as $97, during the initial days of the firesale. As time progresses, the price gradually increases, often by $10 to $30 or more. This pricing cycle continues, enticing buyers to make quick purchasing decisions before the prices rise further.

Firesales are designed to create urgency and scarcity, with a limited number of packages available, usually between 100 to 300 units. This scarcity drives early bird purchases, as buyers understand that once the allotted packages are sold out, the firesale concludes.

Despite the initial investment in creating these packages, often costing several hundred dollars per product, sellers can generate substantial profits during firesales. The combination of limited availability, escalating prices, and high-demand products can result in significant revenue generation within a short timeframe.

For those considering venturing into firesales, starting with a smaller package of five products can provide valuable insights into the operational dynamics. It's essential to modify the private label content to create unique and compelling reports, accompanied by engaging graphics and persuasive sales copy.

Additionally, membership sites present another avenue for generating recurring income using private label rights content. Membership sites offer ongoing value to subscribers by providing a continuous stream of exclusive content, such as articles, reports, and products, sourced from private label rights materials.

Creating a successful membership site involves meticulous planning, including selecting a profitable niche, sourcing high-quality private label rights content, and offering enticing membership packages. By delivering valuable and relevant content consistently, membership sites can attract and retain subscribers, ensuring a steady income stream over time.

Utilizing statistical analysis tools to gauge subscriber interests and preferences can inform content creation strategies, ensuring that the offerings align with the audience's needs and expectations. Offering trial subscriptions and providing exceptional value can further enhance member retention and satisfaction.

While entry-level membership sites may start at lower monthly fees, premium membership sites can command higher prices, provided they deliver substantial value and exclusive content. The key lies in striking the right balance between affordability and value proposition to attract and retain a loyal subscriber base.

Generating ideas for higher-priced membership sites can be achieved by leveraging the private label rights reports and articles from your lower-paying sites. Analyzing the niches that resonate well with your audience in the lower-paying sites can provide valuable insights into potential niches for premium membership offerings.

An often overlooked yet lucrative avenue for maximizing profits from private label rights content is selling your membership sites outright. By leveraging the modified and curated content from each site, you can create unique and original membership sites that hold significant value in the market.

These membership sites encompass various content formats such as e-books, small reports, and other essential resources. The cornerstone of success lies in the uniqueness of your content, as it adds substantial value to your membership sites. The exclusivity of your offerings sets them apart from competitors, making them highly desirable among potential buyers.

Profitability is a direct result of providing real

value and addressing the specific needs of your subscribers through focused content. Your primary goal should always be to cater to the benefit and satisfaction of your members, as their success translates into the success of your membership sites.

Suppose your membership site is consistently earning $2,000 per month. In that case, you can calculate the annual profit and use this figure as a basis for selling your membership site for a substantial five-figure sum. This approach can lead to significant financial gains, especially if you have multiple successful membership sites in your portfolio.

The underlying formula for success remains straightforward: Unique and valuable content combined with profitability equals substantial financial returns. Whether it's through membership sites, e-books, small reports, or video content, your original and high-quality content has the potential to generate substantial revenue streams.

9

Additional Tips About Private Label Rights And Content

When utilizing your private label rights content, it's advisable to minimize the use of images and other elements that might distract from the core message. Customers primarily seek valuable information rather than visual embellishments.

Excessive use of pictures can complicate the process of modifying content and removing them later can be cumbersome. Therefore, it may be more beneficial to avoid including pictures altogether.

When writing or modifying your private label content, adopt the perspective of your target audience—the individuals you intend to sell to. Directing the content towards their needs and interests is crucial for effective communication. Your focus should always be on catering to your customers' requirements.

If your budget permits and time constraints prevent you from creating private label articles, consider hiring a ghostwriter. Platforms like Elance and other freelance writing sites offer a pool of candidates at reasonable rates. You can also explore popular forums to find skilled writers willing to collaborate.

Effective sales letter copy is essential for marketing your products. It should incorporate the following components:

- Headline: A compelling headline in bold red lettering grabs attention and entices readers to explore further.

- Subheadline: This supports the headline, providing additional emphasis on what's to follow.
- Sales Page: Write persuasively as if addressing an individual, highlighting the benefits rather than just listing features.

For instance, if your product addresses challenges related to using private label rights, articulate these issues in your sales letter. Offer solutions and benefits, reassuring potential customers that your product addresses their concerns comprehensively.

In addition, your sales page should specify the format of the product (e.g., PDF, Word document) and detail what customers can do with it (e.g., modify content, create e-courses, newsletters, etc.). Including testimonials enhances credibility, while mentioning limited availability creates a sense of urgency and exclusivity.

Another lucrative avenue is creating software with private label rights. This type of software allows modification and branding according to your specifications, opening doors to diverse market needs and preferences.

Additionally, establishing clear terms and conditions regarding the usage and distribution of your product is crucial. This ensures clarity for customers and protects your intellectual property rights.

Exploring joint ventures, one-time offers (OTOs), and leveraging affiliate programs are also viable strategies for maximizing profits with private label rights content.

By implementing these strategies effectively, you can harness the full potential of private label rights content to build a profitable business efficiently.

Milton Keynes UK
Ingram Content Group UK Ltd.
UKHW051928220424
441543UK00011B/146